HOW TO NAVIGATE LIKE A PRO

Mastering Compass Skill for Adults

Jeanelle K. Douglas

Contents

INTRODUCTION

Introduction Navigating through the woods or even in urban settings may be difficult, especially when relying only on contemporary technology such as GPS. While GPS systems have revolutionized navigation, they are not perfect and can fail for a variety of reasons, including battery depletion, signal loss, and technological problems. In such situations, having a solid backup navigation instrument is critical, and the modest compass shines.

The compass, a simple but powerful tool, has guided explorers, adventurers, and travelers for millennia. Its capacity to point to the magnetic north ensures that navigation remains consistent, independent of technical improvements or environmental variables. Despite its simplicity, many people are unaware of how to properly use a compass. The purpose of this book aims to fill that need by providing a complete reference to compass navigation for adults. This book is for seasoned outdoor enthusiasts, aspiring adventurers, and anybody who wants to feel more secure navigating without relying exclusively on technology. In the following chapters, we will go over the basics of compass navigation, beginning with a grasp of the components of a compass and the distinction between magnetic and true north.

We will look at the fundamental procedures, including orienting the compass, getting bearings, and following a route, to lay the groundwork for effective navigation. Moving beyond the fundamentals, we will delve into map reading essentials, teaching you how to analyze topographic maps and comprehend crucial characteristics like contour lines and grids.

With this understanding, you will be able to combine compass navigation with map reading, improving your navigation abilities in a variety of terrains and conditions. Throughout the book, we'll go over practical navigation techniques like dead reckoning, triangulation, and intersection, so you can navigate effectively even in adverse situations when visible markers may be limited. Furthermore, we'll go over advanced compass abilities like navigating at night, in bad weather, and in specialist domains like aviation and marine navigation. In addition, we'll look at how to combine GPS technology with compass navigation, giving you a diverse toolset for every navigation circumstance. We will cover real-world applications of compass navigation, such as wilderness navigation, orienteering competitions, and geocaching, emphasizing the practicality of compass abilities in a variety of leisure and outdoor activities.

By the end of this book, I hope you will feel not just comfortable but also empowered to travel successfully with a compass in hand. Whether you're going on a backcountry expedition, exploring new territory, or simply looking to improve your outdoor abilities, the information and practices offered here will serve as a compass for success.

So, let us go on this adventure of discovery together and explore the intriguing world of compass navigation. Let the compass be your trusted guide while you navigate the wilderness, find your way through the urban jungle, or simply explore the great outdoors.

Advantages of Navigating with a Compass

Navigation with a compass has several advantages that go beyond merely finding your route from point A to point B.

Here are some of the main advantages:

1. Reliability: Unlike electronic devices such as cellphones or GPS units, which might fail due to battery problems, signal loss, or technical faults, a compass operates only on magnetic principles and is not susceptible to these constraints. It offers a dependable method of navigation, particularly in distant or off-grid areas where other technologies may be problematic.

2. Independence: Learning to navigate with a compass fosters self-reliance and independence. Instead of relying exclusively on technology, you will be able to travel using a simple yet powerful instrument that does not require an external power source. This self-sufficiency is liberating, allowing you to go outside with confidence, knowing you have the ability to travel securely.

3. Versatility: A compass may be utilized in a variety of settings and climates, including deep forests, hilly terrain, deserts, and even cities. It operates in any area where the Earth's magnetic field exists, making it an adaptable navigation aid for a variety of activities like hiking, backpacking, orienteering, geocaching, and wilderness survival.

4. Accuracy: When used correctly, a compass gives precise directional information regardless of external influences like weather or topographical characteristics. It enables you to maintain a steady heading and navigate accurately, even in difficult areas where landmarks may be limited or hidden.

5. Skill Development: To learn the skill of compass navigation, practice, observation, and critical thinking are required. It entails learning principles like magnetic declination, map orientation, and triangulation, as well as practicing practical skills like bearings and following a route. Learning these techniques increases not just your navigational abilities but also your entire outdoor competence and situational awareness.

6. Safety: Navigating using a compass is an important safety skill, particularly in emergency situations where technology may be unavailable or inaccurate. If you become lost or disoriented while participating in outdoor activities, it can assist you with navigating back to safety. Furthermore, including a compass in your essential kit guarantees that you have a dependable navigation tool in the event of an emergency.

7. Connection with Nature: Using a compass to navigate promotes a stronger connection with the natural world. It helps you to pay attention to your surroundings, notice natural characteristics, and have a deeper appreciation for the area. Navigating using a compass helps you connect with your surroundings in a meaningful way, improving your outdoor experience and instilling a sense of stewardship in the natural world. In conclusion, navigating with a compass has several advantages that extend beyond basic direction-finding. It promotes dependability, independence, variety, precision, skill development, safety, and a stronger bond with nature. Mastering compass navigation skills provides you with a critical tool that allows you to confidently and competently explore the outdoors.

UNDERSTANDING THE BASICS

To begin our adventure into the realm of compass navigation, we must first establish a firm foundation by learning the fundamentals of how a compass works and the important rules that govern its operation. A compass is a basic but effective navigating aid that relies on the Earth's magnetic field.

Inside a compass, a magnetic needle aligns with the Earth's magnetic field lines, pointing to the magnetic north pole. This gives you a good reference point for calculating direction. A compass typically consists of several main components, including the magnetic needle, housing, direction of travel arrow, and rotating bezel with degree marks.

Understanding these components and how they interact is critical for successfully utilizing a compass for navigation. One of the most essential ideas in compass navigation is the contrast between magnetic and true north.

True north is the direction toward the geographic North Pole, whereas magnetic north is the direction toward the Earth's magnetic North Pole. This variation, known as magnetic declination, must be considered while navigating with a compass, especially over long distances or in areas with high declination values.

Accurate readings require proper compass calibration. Compass calibration involves aligning the magnetic needle with the north-south axis of the compass housing to correct for any magnetic interference that may affect the accuracy. There are several varieties of compasses available, each with its own unique set of functions and capabilities.

The two main kinds are the baseplate and the Lensatic compass. Baseplate compasses, which include a clear baseplate and a revolving bezel, are popular for general navigation.

Lensatic compasses, on the other hand, are more tough and durable, making them excellent for military use and wilderness survival. In addition to learning the components and operation of a compass, it is critical to learn how to interpret the directional information it provides.

This entails learning cardinal directions (north, south, east, and west) as well as intermediate directions (northeast, southeast, southwest, and northwest) and how to align the compass with these directions.

With a thorough knowledge of these fundamentals, you'll be well-prepared to embark on your trip into the realm of compass navigation.

With this basis established, we can now go further into the practical elements of utilizing a compass for navigation in the following chapters.

What is a compass?

A compass is a navigational tool that determines direction according to the Earth's magnetic poles. It consists of a magnetized needle or card that aligns with the Earth's magnetic field and points to the magnetic North Pole.

This allows users to precisely travel using the cardinal directions (north, south, east, and west). Traditionally, people make a compass by fixing a magnetic needle on a pivot or hanging it in a fluid-filled container that allows it to revolve freely.

Manufacturers frequently mark the needle with one end painted or sculpted to indicate north (usually red or another distinguishing color) and the other end pointing south. To facilitate navigation, compass housings frequently feature degree marks or cardinal direction markers. In addition, modern compasses may include a rotating bezel with degree marks, a map-compatible clear baseplate, and a magnifying lens for examining map details.

Compasses are available in a variety of styles and designs, including:

1. Baseplate compasses: These are popular for general navigation and have a clear baseplate with a revolving bezel for establishing bearings and measuring angles.

2. Lensatic compasses: Also known as military compasses, they are more tough and sturdy, with a hinged cover and sighting mechanism for precision navigation in difficult terrain.

3. Orienteering compasses: Designed primarily for orienteering and navigation activities, these compasses often include a transparent baseplate, bright markings for low-light circumstances, and a spinning bezel with degree marks.

4. Digital compasses: Employ electronic sensors to identify direction and can be included in gadgets like cellphones, GPS units, and watches. Regardless of the kind, a compass is an essential instrument for navigation, especially in outdoor activities like hiking, backpacking, orienteering, and wilderness survival. Its simplicity, dependability, and independence from external power sources make it an invaluable tool for explorers, adventurers, and outdoor lovers alike.

Compass Parts

Many main components make up a compass, each serving a unique purpose in navigation. These components may differ significantly depending on the kind and design of the compass; however, the following are common pieces found in many compasses:

1. Magnetic Needle: The magnetic needle is the most important component of a compass. It is a slender, magnetized needle that aligns with Earth's magnetic field and points to the magnetic North Pole. The needle typically has one end marked to signify north (commonly in red) and the other end indicating south.

2. Housing: The housing is a protective case for the magnetic needle and other internal compass components. It stabilizes and protects the needle, enabling it to rotate freely while retaining its alignment.

3. Baseplate: A flat, clear surface, typically composed of plastic or acrylic. It offers a secure platform for holding the compass and frequently has ruler lines along the borders for measuring distances on a map.

4. Direction-of-Travel Arrow: The compass's baseplate features a fixed arrow or line that indicates the direction of travel. It specifies the direction in which the user should move from one location to another.

5. The revolving bezel: Is a circular ring that surrounds the magnetic needle. Around its circle, degree markers (0° to 360°) or cardinal direction signs (N, S, E, and W) are usually present. Users can rotate the bezel to point in a specific direction or bearing, enabling them to calculate their heading or plot a path.

6. Orienting Lines or Arrow: Some compasses have orienting lines or an orienting arrow on their baseplates.

These marks help to align the compass with the map while taking bearings or navigating with a map and compass.

7. Index Line or Index Pointer: The index line or index pointer is a fixed line or notch that runs down the edge of the compass housing. It works in conjunction with the magnetic needle to calculate the compass's direction or bearing.

8. Declination Adjustment: Some compasses have a declination adjustment mechanism that allows the user to account for the difference between magnetic north and true north (known as magnetic declination) at their unique location. These are the basic components of a compass that are common in most designs. Familiarizing yourself with these components and their roles is critical to successfully utilizing a compass for navigation.

MAGNETIC NORTH VS. TRUE NORTH MAGNETIC NORTH VS. TRUE NORTH

Understanding the distinction between magnetic north and true north is essential for proper compass navigation. **Magnetic North:** The magnetic north is the direction that a compass needle's north-seeking pole points in. The flow of molten iron in the planet's outer core determines the Earth's magnetic field. The magnetic north pole is close to the geographic North Pole but not precisely aligned with it.

The Earth's magnetic field is not uniform, varying in intensity and direction throughout its surface. This change, known as magnetic declination, causes the magnetic needle of a compass to stray slightly from true north. Magnetic North serves as a reference point for compass navigation, allowing users to establish their orientation relative to Magnetic North and travel successfully using a compass.

True North: True north, also known as geographic north, is the direction to the geographic North Pole, the northernmost point on Earth's surface.

True north symbolizes the Earth's axis of rotation, which is parallel to the Earth's longitude meridians. True north, unlike magnetic north, is a permanent point on the Earth's surface that remains constant regardless of magnetic changes or geographic location. It acts as a reference point for map orientation and celestial navigation.

The difference between magnetic north and true north, known as magnetic declination, varies with geographic location and might be positive, negative, or zero. In certain places, magnetic north and true north coincide completely, yielding zero declination. In some regions, the difference might be many degrees, necessitating changes to compass readings to account for the declination.

To ensure precise navigation, it is critical to account for magnetic declination when using a compass. Navigators who grasp the distinction between magnetic north and true north may modify their compass readings and navigate efficiently in any geographic region.

Compass Calibration

Compass calibration is an important step in ensuring that a compass is accurate and reliable for navigation. Calibration is the process of aligning a compass's magnetic needle with the Earth's magnetic field to adjust for any extraneous variables that may impair its accuracy.

Here's a full description of compass calibration:

A compass's magnetic needle may become misaligned as a result of exposure to magnetic fields or mechanical stress during manufacturing or storage. As a result, the needle may not point precisely to magnetic north, resulting in inaccurate readings and navigation mistakes. To calibrate a compass, start by holding it level and stable in your palm, making sure it is not near any metal items or electrical gadgets that may interfere with the magnetic needle. Next, rotate the compass horizontally in a full circle several times to let the magnetic needle settle and align with the Earth's magnetic field. Once the magnetic needle has steadied, spin the compass housing until the needle's north-seeking end corresponds to the compass housing's orienting arrow or north indication. This step ensures that the compass is properly oriented and calibrated to magnetic north. In addition to horizontal calibration, some compasses may require vertical calibration to assure accuracy in various orientations. To do vertical calibration, hold the compass vertically with the magnetic needle facing upwards, and rotate it repeatedly to allow the needle to settle and align with the Earth's magnetic field.

After calibrating the compass, it is critical to check the accuracy of the readings must be checked for accuracy by comparing them to known landmarks or map features. The compass is fully calibrated and ready for use if the readings are consistent and match the predicted directions.

Regular calibration of the compass is necessary, particularly when exposed to high magnetic fields, severe temperatures, or mechanical stress. Regular calibration helps preserve the compass's accuracy and dependability, allowing for precise navigation in any circumstance. Navigators may rely on their compasses as trusted instruments for precise and reliable outdoor navigation by following suitable calibration methods and testing the accuracy of the compass readings on a regular basis.

THE FUNDAMENTALS OF COMPASS NAVIGATION

Compass navigation is built on a few essential principles that serve as the foundation for successful navigation. Understanding the fundamentals is critical for navigating properly and comfortably in any context.

1. **Orienting the Compass:** To guarantee reliable readings, orient the compass by aligning its housing with the Earth's magnetic field. To orient the compass, keep it level and steady, away from any metal items or electrical gadgets that might interfere with the magnetic needle. Next, spin the compass housing until the magnetic needle's north-seeking end coincides with the orienting arrow or north indication. Orienting the compass ensures it is properly aligned and ready for navigation.

2. **Taking a bearing:** Taking a bearing means identifying the direction of an item or landmark in relation to your current location. To take a bearing, keep the compass level and steady, and point the direction-of-travel arrow or sighting notch toward

the item or landmark you want to navigate to. Next, spin the compass housing until the magnetic needle lines up with the orienting arrow or north indication. The degree marker on the rotating bezel, where the magnetic needle aligns, indicates the item's bearing or direction.

3. **Following A Bearing:** Following a bearing entails walking or traveling in the direction indicated by the compass bearing. To follow a bearing, keep the compass level and steady, and ensure that the magnetic needle remains aligned with the orienting arrow or north indication. Keep the direction-of-travel arrow or sighting notch pointed in the direction of the bearing as you navigate to your destination, checking the compass every now and then to ensure you're on track.

4. **Setting a Course:** Setting a course entails determining a precise path or direction of travel toward a goal. Setting a course involves determining the intended bearing or direction of travel to your destination using a map or other navigation aids. Next, adjust the compass's rotating bezel until the

desired bearing corresponds to the orienting arrow or the north indication. The direction-of-travel arrow or sighting notch should now point in the direction of your desired path. Use this path to get to your destination, changing your direction as necessary to stay on track.

Mastering these compass navigation essentials will allow you to confidently navigate in any situation, whether you're hiking through dense forests, traversing over vast plains, or exploring rocky mountain terrain. Compass navigation improves with practice and expertise, allowing you to explore with confidence and precision.

Orienting the Compass

Orienting the compass is an essential stage in compass navigation, ensuring accurate readings and precise navigation. When you orient the compass, you line the housing with the Earth's magnetic field, causing the magnetic needle to point to the magnetic north. This method creates the proper reference point for establishing direction and getting precise bearings.

To orient the compass, first hold it level and stable in your palm, making sure it is not near any metal items or other gadgets that might interfere with the magnetic needle. Next, spin the compass housing until the magnetic needle's north-seeking end coincides with the orienting arrow or north indication.

This alignment guarantees that the compass housing faces magnetic north, allowing the magnetic needle to travel freely and properly indicate direction. When the magnetic needle aligns with the pointing arrow, the compass is correctly oriented and ready to navigate.

Orienting the compass is an important step to take before getting bearings or establishing courses. Without adequate orientation, compass readings might be erroneous, resulting in navigation mistakes and confusion. By making the effort to properly align the compass, you guarantee that your navigation is based on trustworthy and precise directional information, allowing you to travel confidently and successfully in any setting.

Taking a Bearing

Using a compass to take a bearing is a fundamental navigation skill that allows you to identify the direction of an item or landmark in relation to your current position. Align the compass with the objective and read the angle or bearing provided by the compass needle.

Here's a full description of how to take a bearing:

Begin by holding the compass level and steady in your hand, making sure it is not near any metal items or electrical equipment that might interfere with the magnetic needle. Identify the item or landmark you want to navigate to, then aim the compass's direction-of-travel arrow or sighting notch at it.

Next, spin the compass housing until the magnetic needle matches the orienting arrow or north indicator on the housing. The degree marker on the rotating bezel, where the magnetic needle aligns, indicates the item's bearing or direction.

To calculate the object's bearing, look for the degree marker on the revolving bezel. The degree measurement indicates the angle between the magnetic north and the direction of the item. For example, if the magnetic needle coincides with the bezel's 30-degree marker, the bearing on the item is 30 degrees from the magnetic north.

The compass bearing relative to magnetic north may need correction for magnetic declination to achieve true north. Depending on your geographical location, you may need to add or subtract the declination value from the compass bearing to get the correct bearing for the item.

To take accurate bearings, you must have steady hands, position the compass carefully, and practice. Mastering the ability to get bearings will allow you to confidently and accurately navigate towards specific objects or landmarks, improving your general navigation abilities in any outdoor area.

Following a Bearing

Taking a bearing is a key skill in compass navigation that allows you to identify the direction of an item or landmark in relation to your current position. It entails aligning the compass with the intended destination and reading the degree marker on the compass bezel, where the magnetic needle points. This degree indication denotes the angle or bearing between your current position and the objective.

To take a bearing, first hold the compass level and steady in your hand, making sure it is not near any metal items or electrical gadgets that may interfere with the magnetic needle. Next, aim the compass's direction-of-travel arrow or sighting notch toward the item or landmark you want to navigate to.

After aligning the compass with the objective, spin the compass housing until the magnetic needle matches the orienting arrow or north indication on the compass housing. The degree marker on the revolving bezel, where the magnetic needle aligns, indicates the bearing or direction to the target.

To calculate the bearing to the target, refer to the degree marker on the bezel. This bearing depicts the angle between your current position and the target, measured in degrees clockwise from magnetic north. For example, if the magnetic needle matches the 60-degree marker on the bezel, the bearing to the target is 60 degrees from magnetic north.

Taking a bearing helps you establish a directional reference point and properly travel to your intended location. Mastering this talent allows you to successfully navigate across a variety of terrains and surroundings, ensuring that you stay on track and arrive at your goal safely and effectively.

Setting a Course

Setting a course is an important part of compass navigation because it involves arranging a precise path or direction of travel to reach a destination. It allows you to establish a distinct heading or bearing towards your desired destination, directing you along the correct path.

To set a course with a compass, first determine the intended bearing or direction of travel to your destination. Using a map or other navigation aids, you may determine the azimuth or angle between your present position and the destination.

After you've calculated the required bearing, keep the compass level and steady in your palm, away from any metal objects or electrical gadgets that may interfere with the magnetic needle. Next, adjust the compass's rotating bezel until the desired bearing corresponds to the orienting arrow or north indication on the compass housing.

The compass's direction-of-travel arrow or sighting notch should now point in the direction you plan to go. This specifies the heading or bearing that you must take to reach your destination.

With the compass's route established, you may confidently travel along the chosen path, changing your heading as needed to stay on track. Check the compass on a regular basis to confirm that you are on the right track and getting closer to your goal.

Setting a route helps you set a clear path of travel and navigate more effectively to your destination. Mastering this ability allows you to confidently plan and execute your navigation strategy, ensuring that you arrive at your target location safely and effectively.

MAP READING ESSENTIALS

Map reading is a crucial skill in navigation that entails analyzing and comprehending the information on a map. Whether you're exploring new territory, planning a hike, or navigating in the outdoors, map reading is critical for precise navigation and route planning.

Here are the important map reading essentials:

Map Symbols and Features: Maps have a wide range of symbols and features that depict natural and man-made landmarks, terrain types, flora, bodies of water, and other geographical elements. Understanding these symbols is critical for comprehending the map's information and recognizing major landmarks and features in the surrounding area.

Scale and Orientation: Maps are rendered to scale, indicating the connection between map distances and ground distances. Map scales are often shown as a ratio or graphical scale bar. Understanding the scale enables you to estimate distances precisely and plan your travel appropriately. Maps are also oriented to line with the cardinal directions (north, south, east, and west), allowing you to establish the direction of travel and properly orient the map.

Contour Lines: Contour lines are a key component of topographic maps, representing variations in elevation and landscape relief. Contour lines link points of equal height, creating a set of lines that represent the terrain's shape and properties. Understanding contour lines allows you to see the landscape and recognize characteristics like hills, valleys, ridges, and depressions on a map.

Map Grids and Coordinates: Maps are frequently split into grids and labeled with coordinates to aid navigation and location identification. Grid lines, such as latitude and longitude lines or Universal Transverse Mercator (UTM) grid lines, are a systematic method for dividing the map into smaller portions and pinpointing specific places using coordinates. Understanding map grids and coordinates enables you to precisely pinpoint points on a map and convey your location to others.

Map Legend: The map legend, also known as the key, offers a reference for deciphering the symbols and characteristics depicted on the map. It defines the meaning of map symbols, colors, and other graphical components found on maps. The map legend helps you recognize and comprehend the numerous symbols and characteristics represented on the map.

Scale Bar: The scale bar is a graphical depiction of the map scale that shows the link between map distances and ground distances. The scale bar allows you to precisely measure distances and estimate travel times between locations on the map.

Mastering these map-reading skills will allow you to confidently interpret and navigate, ensuring that you remain on track and arrive at your destination safely and quickly. Map reading is a useful ability that will help you enjoy your outdoor experiences and confidently explore and navigate the globe.

Map Symbols and Features

Maps include a variety of symbols and elements to depict natural and man-made landmarks, terrain types, flora, bodies of water, and other geographical characteristics. Understanding these symbols is critical for correctly reading the information on the map and navigating in a variety of contexts. Here are some often-used map symbols and features:

Natural features

Mountains: contour lines or darkened patches represent elevation and landscape relief. Peaks and summits are frequently linked to elevation values.

Valleys: Contoured or shaded regions between mountain ridges indicate lower altitudes and landscape depressions.

Rivers and Streams: blue lines with arrows showing direction of flow. The line's width may vary depending on the size of the water body.

Lakes and Ponds: Blue-shaded regions or outlines indicate bodies of water. The size and form of the darkened region or outline vary with the size and shape of the water body. Forests and Wooded Areas: Green-shaded areas or symbols indicate regions covered in trees and other vegetation.

Man-made Features

Roads and Highways: Black or gray lines of variable widths indicate the various types of roads (e.g., highways, secondary roads, dirt roads).

Railroads: shown as black lines with parallel lines or crosshatches denoting railway tracks.

Buildings and Structures: Black squares, rectangles, or symbols depict buildings, homes, bridges, towers, and other man-made structures.

Boundaries: Solid or dashed lines represent political boundaries such as nation borders, state/province boundaries, and administrative boundaries.

Trails and Footpaths: Dashed or dotted lines indicate hiking trails, footpaths, and recreational pathways.

Geographic features:

Contour Lines: lines linking sites of equal height that depict variations in landscape relief and elevation. Contour lines show the ground's form and steepness.

Elevation Points: labeled points on the map denoting specific altitudes, usually found on mountain peaks, summits, or other noteworthy areas.

Spot Elevations: numerical values that represent particular elevations at various spots on the map.

Point of Interest Symbols:

Campsites: Tent icons indicate authorized camping spaces. Picnic places: Picnic table icons represent authorized picnic places.

Lookouts and vistas: Binocular icons represent picturesque vistas or observation sites.

Historical Sites: Symbols represent historical landmarks, monuments, ruins, or archeological sites.

These are only a handful of the many symbols and features available on maps. Familiarizing yourself with these symbols and knowing their meanings is critical for successful map reading and navigation in a variety of outdoor settings.

Understanding Contour Lines

Understanding contour lines is critical for comprehending topographic maps and visualizing the topographical characteristics shown on them. Contour lines are essential components of topographic maps, representing variations in height and landscape relief.

Here's a full description of contour lines and how to read them:

Definition: Contour lines are imaginary lines on a map that link places of equal height above a reference point, such as sea level. Each contour line represents a distinct elevation, while the distance between contour lines reflects the slope of the landscape.

Interpretation:

Elevation: Contour lines show variations in elevation, with each line indicating a distinct elevation above or below a reference point. Surveyors frequently label the numerical value of the elevation on or near the contour line to show the elevation of that specific line.

Terrain Relief: The spacing and arrangement of contour lines indicate the terrain relief and slope of the land. Closely spaced contour lines denote steep terrain, whereas widely spread contour lines denote mild slopes or level land. Contour lines typically show a continuous height difference between them across the map and are displayed in the map legend.

Topographic Features: Contour lines produce a variety of patterns and forms to depict topographic features such as hills, valleys, ridges, and depressions. For example: **Hills:** Circular or concentric contour lines with greater altitudes in the center denote hills or peaks. The contour lines get more closely spaced as they reach the hill's crest. **Valleys:** Contour lines that create V-shaped patterns with decreasing altitudes toward the center denote valleys or depressions. The contour lines grow more closely spaced as they descend into the valley.

Ridges: contour lines that form U-shaped patterns with greater heights toward the center denote ridges or spurs. As one ascends along the ridge, the contour lines get closer together.

Depressions: Contour lines that create closed loops or

circles with lower altitudes indicate depressions, which can be basins, craters, or sinkholes.

Index Contour Lines: These are thicker or darker contour lines with elevation values indicated. These lines often appear at regular intervals (e.g., every fifth contour line) and serve as reference points for evaluating the terrain's height and slope.

Understanding Gradient: The space between contour lines determines the terrain's gradient or slope. Closely placed contour lines indicate steeper slopes, whereas widely spread contour lines suggest softer slopes. Analyzing the arrangement and spacing of contour lines allows you to visualize the land's slope and plan your approach appropriately.

Overall, understanding contour lines is critical for reading topographic maps and picturing the topographical elements depicted on them. By examining the height, spacing, and arrangement of contour lines, you may learn about the area's terrain and navigate comfortably in a variety of outdoor conditions.

SCALE AND ORIENTATION

Scale

Scale is a key component of maps that reflects the connection between distances on the map and distances on the ground. Cartographers create maps to scale to accurately portray geographical features and distances. Map scales are often depicted as a ratio (e.g., 1:50,000) or a graphical scale bar.

A ratio scale specifies that one unit of measurement on the map equals a specific number of units of measurement on the ground. A 1:50,000 scale, for example, indicates that one unit of measurement on the map (e.g., 1 inch) corresponds to 50,000 units of measurement on the ground (e.g., 50,000 inches or 0.79 miles). The smaller the ratio's denominator, the greater the map's scale and detail.

Segments divide a line in a graphical scale bar, with each representing a specific ground distance. Users may better estimate journey durations and distances by comparing the length of the scale bar to the appropriate ground distance.

Orientation

Orientation is the alignment of a map with the cardinal directions (north, south, east, and west) to facilitate precise navigation and understanding of directional data. Maps are oriented to correspond with the cardinal directions, giving users a constant reference point for identifying direction.

A compass rose or arrow indicating the direction of north relative to the map often indicates the map's orientation. To give extra navigational reference points, the compass rose may contain cardinal directions (N, S, E, and W) as well as intermediate directions (NE, SE, SW, and NW).

When utilizing a map for navigation, it is critical to align the map with the cardinal directions to guarantee an appropriate interpretation of directional data. This enables users to establish their direction and navigate efficiently to their chosen destination.

Map users who understand size and orientation can properly assess distances, estimate journey durations, and confidently navigate in a variety of contexts.

These characteristics are required for good map reading and navigation, allowing users to plan routes, recognize landmarks, and arrive safely and efficiently.

Map Grids and Coordinates

Map grids and coordinates are critical components of maps because they provide a methodical way to split the map into smaller portions and identify individual places using accurate coordinates. They let users properly pinpoint points on a map, convey their location to others, and navigate efficiently in a variety of settings.

Here's a full explanation of map grids and coordinates:

Map grids

Map grids are a network of imaginary lines superimposed on a map to split it into smaller portions for easier navigation and location reference.

There are several common types of map grids, including:

1. The Latitude and Longitude Grid divides the earth's surface into a network of horizontal latitude and vertical longitude lines. Latitude lines go east-west

and measure distances north and south of the equator, whereas longitude lines run north-south and measure east and west of the prime meridian. The intersection of latitude and longitude lines results in a grid coordinate, which allows users to identify precise areas on the map.

2. The Universal Transverse Mercator (UTM) Grid splits the Earth's surface into zones, each with its own coordinate system based on the transverse Mercator projection. Easting and northing coordinates in the UTM grid are measured in meters and denote the distance east and north from the origin of each UTM zone. UTM coordinates are a precise and standardized approach to finding points on a map, particularly for large-scale mapping and military applications.

3. The Military Grid Reference System (MGRS) is a version of the UTM grid that military organizations utilize for accurate position reference and navigation. It splits the Earth's surface into smaller grids using alphanumeric grid coordinates, allowing users to identify places more accurately and precisely.

MGRS coordinates include a grid zone designator, a grid square identifier, and numerical coordinates inside the grid square.

Coordinates

Coordinates are numerical numbers that describe a point's exact position on a map. Latitude and longitude, or easting and northing coordinates commonly represent them, depending on the grid system used. Coordinates provide a standard and widely accepted method of communicating and referencing map places.

Latitude and longitude coordinates are represented in degrees, minutes, and seconds (DMS) or decimal degrees (DD), signifying the angular distance north or south of the equator and east or west of the prime meridian, respectively. Latitude values vary from 0° at the equator to 90° north or south at the poles, whereas longitude values range from 0° at the prime meridian to 180° east or west at the International Date Line.

Measure easting and northing coordinates in meters to denote distances east and north of a reference point inside the grid system, such as the origin of a UTM zone or the southwest corner of a grid square in MGRS. Easting coordinates grow to the east, while northing coordinates rise to the north, offering an accurate and consistent method for locating points on a map.

Understanding map grids and coordinates allows users to precisely find positions on a map, convey their location to others, and travel efficiently in a variety of contexts. These characteristics are required for accurate map reading, navigation, and location reference, allowing users to plan routes, recognize landmarks, and arrive at their destinations with confidence.

PRACTICAL NAVIGATION TECHNIQUES

Practical navigation strategies include a variety of approaches and abilities for navigating efficiently in external contexts. These approaches are critical for hikers, trekkers, sailors, and outdoor enthusiasts who rely on maps, compasses, and other navigational aids to navigate new territory.

Here are some useful navigational techniques:

1. Map Reading: The ability to read maps is essential for outdoor navigation. It entails reading and comprehending the data shown on a map, such as symbols, contours, scale, and direction. You can recognize landmarks, plan routes, and navigate successfully in varied terrains if you are familiar with a map's characteristics and understand how to interpret them.

2. Compass Navigation: Compass navigation is another important ability for outdoor navigation. It entails using a compass to find direction, take bearings, and plot courses. By aligning the compass with the cardinal directions and getting the correct bearings, you may navigate with precision and accuracy, even in locations where landmarks are not visible.

3. Terrain Association: Terrain association is a navigation strategy that includes matching elements on the map to their corresponding terrain characteristics in the area. By recognizing notable landmarks, topographical contours, and natural features such as hills, valleys, and water bodies, you may navigate by comparing what you see on the map to what you see in the terrain.

4. Dead Reckoning: Dead reckoning is a navigation strategy that includes guessing your position using your prior known location, direction of travel, and distance traveled. Keeping track of your direction and distance traveled from a known location allows you to estimate your present position on the map and navigate appropriately.

4. **Pacing and Timing:** Pacing and timing are approaches for measuring distances and estimating trip times when traveling on foot. Counting your steps and knowing your average pace allows you to determine the distance traveled and plan your journey appropriately. Similarly, assessing your travel speed and knowing the distance to your goal allows you to predict the time it will take to arrive.

6. **Celestial Navigation:** Celestial navigation uses celestial bodies like the sun, moon, stars, and planets to identify direction and navigate. Observing the position of celestial bodies relative to the horizon and employing specialist equipment such as a sextant can help you establish your position and direction of travel, especially when other navigational aids are unavailable.

7. **GPS Navigation:** Global Positioning System (GPS) navigation uses GPS receivers to establish your exact location using satellite signals. GPS devices give precise positional information, such as latitude, longitude, and altitude, allowing you to travel with confidence in any situation. However, it

is critical to have a backup strategy in case of a GPS signal loss or gadget failure.

Mastering these practical navigation strategies will allow you to travel comfortably and successfully in outdoor conditions, ensuring that you arrive at your destination securely and efficiently. Whether you're hiking over challenging terrain, sailing across vast oceans, or exploring distant wilderness regions, these abilities will help you navigate with confidence and precision.

Using a Compass and a Map

Using a compass and a map is an essential skill for successful navigation in outdoor conditions. By combining map information with a compass's directional skills, you can properly establish your position, plan routes, and reliably arrive at your destination.

Here's a full explanation of how to use a compass with a map:

1. Orienting the Map: Before using a compass with a map, it is critical to align the map with the cardinal directions (north, south, east, and west). You may accomplish this by matching the map's edge with your compass's magnetic north orientation. Alternatively, you may utilize terrain features or landmarks to match the map to the surrounding landscape.

2. Identifying Landmarks: Use the map to locate notable landmarks, topographical features, and other reference points in the immediate vicinity. Look for landmarks like mountain peaks, rivers, highways, and trails to help you find your position and plan your trip.

3. Taking a Bearing: Locate the direction of your preferred path or destination on a map. To get a bearing, line the edge of the compass baseplate with your current position and the destination on the map. Rotate the compass housing until the orienting arrow or north indication lines up with the magnetic needle.

4. Following the Bearing: Once you've taken a bearing, keep the compass level and stable in your hand, making sure that the direction-of-travel arrow or sighting notch points in the same direction as the bearing. Use the compass to guide your travels, checking it on a regular basis to ensure you're on the right track.

5. Navigating to Waypoints: If you have identified specific waypoints or landmarks along your path, use the compass to go to each one by obtaining bearings from your present location to the waypoints on the map. To get from one waypoint to the next, follow the compass bearings, changing your heading as needed to stay on track.

6. Checking Progress: Check your progress on the

map by comparing your present position to the intended path and checkpoints. Use terrain features and landmarks to confirm your location and ensure you're on the right track.

7. Adjusting for Declination: In areas with significant magnetic declination, you may need to adjust your compass readings to account for the difference between magnetic and true north. By consulting the map or declination information.

DEAD RECKONING

Dead reckoning is a navigation technique that estimates your current position based on your previous known position, direction of travel, and distance traveled. It is an important skill for navigating in outdoor settings where landmarks may be scarce or visibility is limited.

Here's a detailed explanation of how to use dead reckoning.

To begin, locate your starting point on the map using identifiable landmarks or GPS coordinates. This is your initial, known position.

Next, determine your intended direction of travel. You can determine this with a compass or by identifying a visible landmark in the direction you want to go.

Keep track of the distance traveled as you set out on your adventure. You can estimate the distance traveled based on your pace, count your steps, or use a GPS device or pedometer.

Continuously monitor your direction of travel to ensure that you maintain a consistent heading. Use visual cues, such as prominent landmarks or terrain features, to help you stay on course.

As you progress along your intended route, periodically estimate your current position based on your previous known position, direction of travel, and distance traveled. Mark your estimated position on the map and adjust your course accordingly.

Be aware of factors that may affect your dead reckoning calculations, such as changes in terrain, elevation, or weather conditions. To account for these factors and ensure accuracy in your navigation, adjust your estimates as needed.

If possible, periodically verify your estimated position by identifying visible landmarks or terrain features that match those depicted on the map. This helps confirm that you are on the correct route and allows you to make any necessary adjustments to your navigation plan.

Continue to use dead reckoning to navigate to your intended destination, adjusting your course and estimating your position as needed based on your progress and changing conditions.

You can navigate confidently and effectively in outdoor environments using dead reckoning, even when landmarks are scarce or visibility is limited. Practice this skill in various terrains and conditions to improve your navigation abilities and enhance your outdoor adventures.

Triangulation

Triangulation is a navigation technique that uses bearings to calculate your exact location in relation to two or more recognized landmarks or reference points. It calculates your position using geometric and trigonometric concepts, based on intersecting lines of sight from known landmarks.

Land navigation, sea navigation, and surveying all make use of triangulation.

Here's a full explanation of how triangulation works.

1. Identifying Landmarks: To utilize triangulation, you must first identify at least two recognized landmarks or reference points on the map that are visible from your current position. These landmarks should be clearly identifiable and have different characteristics that allow you to precisely establish their location.

2. Taking Bearings : Using a compass or other navigational equipment, take bearings to each recognized landmark from your current position. Measure the angle clockwise from a reference direction, usually magnetic or true north, to the direction of the landmark. To avoid inaccuracies in your computations, make sure you take the correct bearing measurements.

3. Plotting Bearings: After taking bearings to recognized landmarks, use a protractor or compass to transfer them on the map. Draw lines on the map to show each bearing's direction from your current location to the known landmarks. These are known as "lines of position" or "bearing lines."

4. Line Intersection: The spot on the map where the bearing lines connect is your approximate location. The more exact your bearings are and the greater the distance between the landmarks, the more accurate your projected position will be. Triangulation operates on the assumption that your true location is where the lines of your position cross.

5. Adjustments: If the bearings are not perfectly correct or the placement of the landmarks is unknown, you may need to change your estimated position. You may improve your estimated location by obtaining additional bearings on other landmarks or reference points and changing the position until the lines connect more precisely.

6. Verification: After calculating your estimated position with triangulation, you must verify it by comparing it to other features on the map or using other navigation techniques. To validate the accuracy of your estimated position, search for local landmarks, geographical features, or geographic coordinates.

7. Practical Considerations: Keep in mind that topographical features, barriers, and magnetic declination can all affect triangulation, introducing mistakes into your computations. Practice triangulation in a variety of situations and conditions to improve your abilities and accuracy.

Triangulation allows you to precisely locate yourself in the field, even in locations where GPS signals are missing or unreliable. Triangulation is a useful navigation method that improves your ability to navigate safely and successfully in outdoor settings.

Intersection

Intersection, also known as triangulation, is a navigation technique that determines your current position on a map by taking bearings from at least two known landmarks or features. This approach works on the assumption that your position is where the lines of sight from your location to the recognized landmarks connect or cross on the map.

To execute the intersection:

1. Determine at least two notable landmarks or characteristics that are visible from your current position and easily identifiable on a map. Position these landmarks a sufficient distance apart and ensure they have distinguishing characteristics that make them easily visible on a map.

2. Using a compass, take bearings on each of the indicated landmarks from your current position. To do so, aim the compass's direction-of-travel arrow or sighting notch toward the landmark and spin the housing until the magnetic needle aligns with the orienting arrow or north indication.

3. Record the bearings to each landmark by noting the degree markings on the compass bezel or calculating the angle created by the line of sight to the landmark and the direction of magnetic north.

4. To transfer the bearings to the map, draw or extend lines of sight from your current location to each of the

listed landmarks. Ensure the lines align precisely with the compass bearings.

5. Repeat the process for the second landmark, creating a new line or extending your current line of sight to the second point on the map.

6. On the map, your estimated current position is where the lines indicating the bearings to the two landmarks connect or cross. The accuracy of the intersection method depends on several criteria, such as the accuracy of the bearings used, the visibility of the landmarks, and the precision with which the lines are drawn on the map. As a result, it is critical to collect precise bearings, locate dependable landmarks, and carefully transfer the bearings to the map to guarantee that the projected position is correct.

Intersection is a useful navigation technique that, when combined with other methods like dead reckoning and map reading, may help you identify your position and travel efficiently in outdoor conditions. Use this strategy in a variety of terrains and circumstances to improve your navigation abilities and outdoor excursions.

Advanced Compass Skills

Advanced compass abilities include a variety of approaches and strategies that extend beyond the fundamental use of a compass for navigation. These abilities are critical for seasoned outdoor enthusiasts, navigators, and explorers who want to travel more correctly and successfully in difficult terrain.

Here's a full breakdown of advanced compass skills:

1. Precise Bearings: Advanced compass users may utilize precise bearings to navigate more accurately. This includes keeping the compass stable and level and reducing mistakes caused by tilt or movement. By acquiring exact bearings, navigators may estimate directions more precisely, allowing for more accurate navigation along specified routes.

2. Back Bearings: Navigators take back bearings in the opposite direction of travel to validate their position and progress along a route. Advanced compass users may take back bearings by aligning the compass with a

familiar landmark behind them and recording the compass needle's opposite direction. This strategy is notably useful for validating position when doing difficult navigation activities or retracing steps along a route.

3. Aiming Off: Aiming off is a navigation approach that involves purposely deviating slightly from the intended location. Navigating to a linear feature, such as a path or river, involves using this strategy. By aiming slightly to the side of the feature, navigators may assure themselves that they reach it even if they deviate from their original goal. Strategic aiming helps advanced compass users navigate more effectively and reduce the risk of becoming disoriented.

4. Resection: Resection is a strategy for determining your present location on a map by getting bearings from at least two known landmarks or features. Advanced compass users can execute resection correctly and swiftly, helping them to more precisely locate their location on the map. This strategy is especially beneficial

when traveling in low-visibility terrain or when you're unsure of your actual location.

5. Night Navigation: Advanced compass users are skilled in night navigation techniques, which enable them to navigate efficiently in low-light or overnight circumstances. This might include utilizing luminous or lit compasses, techniques like star navigation or celestial navigation, and alternate means for orienting the compass and taking bearings in the dark.

6. Declination Adjustment: Advanced compass users know how to compensate for magnetic declination, which is the angular difference between magnetic north and true north. Navigators can verify that their compass readings correspond to the real direction of travel displayed on the chart by using the proper declination adjustment. This competence is required for precise navigation over long distances and in places with substantial declination.

7. Terrain Association with Compass: Advanced compass users employ terrain association techniques in conjunction with compass navigation to better negotiate

difficult terrain. Navigators may confidently and correctly navigate complicated landscapes by matching map items with equivalent terrain characteristics in the surroundings and utilizing the compass to check directions and bearings.

8. Compass Calibration and Maintenance: Advanced compass users recognize the need for compass calibration and maintenance to ensure precise navigation. They understand how to correctly calibrate their compasses, account for inaccuracies, and ensure that they are in excellent working order. This includes inspecting, cleaning, and adjusting the compass on a regular basis to ensure navigational accuracy and dependability.

Superior compass abilities need much practice, expertise, and a thorough comprehension of navigational concepts. Mastering these strategies allows experienced outdoor enthusiasts and navigators to navigate comfortably and successfully in demanding terrain, ensuring safe and successful outdoor activities.

Navigation in a Difficult Terrain

Advanced abilities and tactics are required for safe and successful navigation over harsh landscapes, dense woods, hilly regions, and other tough terrain.

Here's a full summary of navigation strategies designed particularly for tough terrain:

1. Terrain Association: Terrain association is a fundamental navigation approach that includes matching elements on the map to their corresponding terrain characteristics in the area. In difficult terrain, such as thick woods or hilly areas, terrain association is much more important. Navigators must recognize major landmarks, terrain contours, ridgelines, valleys, and other natural features in order to establish their location and plan their path.

2. Path Planning and Analysis: Before heading into difficult terrain, carefully plan and evaluate your path. Examine the topographic map to discover potential barriers, dangers, and tough terrain characteristics along your proposed path. In the event of an emergency or

unforeseen roadblock, plan alternative routes or escape routes. Consider elevation gain, slope steepness, water supplies, and visibility while designing your route.

3. Navigation by Bearings: Using a compass to acquire exact bearings is critical when navigating in difficult terrain where landmarks may be rare or vision is limited. Take precise bearings on notable landmarks or objects visible in the area, and use them to navigate your intended path. Back bearings are extremely important for determining your position and tracking your progress throughout the journey.

4. Dead Reckoning: Dead reckoning is the process of determining your current position using your prior known position, direction of travel, and distance traveled. In difficult terrain with little sight, dead reckoning can be an effective navigation strategy. Keep track of your route, mileage traveled, and topographical characteristics encountered to determine your present position on the map.

5. Pacing and Timing: When traveling on foot, pacing and timing are techniques for measuring distances and

estimating trip times. Pacing and timing are especially critical when assessing progress and planning navigation legs in difficult terrain. Maintain a regular speed, monitor your trip time to estimate the distance traveled, and plan your itinerary accordingly.

6. Using Handrails and Catch Features: Handrails are linear terrain features that can help you navigate difficult terrain. Examples include rivers, ridgelines, footpaths, and roadways. Handrails can help you navigate and maintain a constant direction of travel. Catch features are notable terrain features along your chosen path that might act as reference markers or safety signs. Identify catch points throughout your trip to help you remain on track and travel safely.

7. Adapting to changing conditions: Challenging terrain frequently presents unpredictable and changeable conditions, such as weather, terrain impediments, and navigational issues. Navigators must be prepared to alter their navigation tactics and plans in response to changing situations. To travel safely and efficiently, maintain flexibility, alertness, and responsiveness to changes in

the terrain and surroundings. Outdoor lovers and explorers who learn these tough terrain navigation skills will be able to navigate confidently and securely through harsh landscapes, dense woods, hilly regions, and other difficult terrain. To increase your navigation abilities and outdoor experiences, practice these skills in a variety of demanding locations.

Night Navigation Using a Compass

Night navigation using a compass is a specialized ability that enables outdoor enthusiasts and navigators to travel safely and successfully in low-light or nighttime settings. While traveling at night brings unique obstacles, such as poor sight and depth perception, utilizing a compass can aid in maintaining directional alignment and correct navigation. Here's a full discussion of night navigation with a compass:

1. Preparation: Before starting on a night navigation adventure, careful planning is required. During daylight hours, familiarize yourself with the area and route to identify notable landmarks, topographical features, and potential risks. Make sure you have a dependable compass with bright or lighted markings to help you navigate in low-light settings. Also, pack a lantern or flashlight with sufficient batteries to illuminate the compass and map as required.

2. Orientation: For night navigation, establishing an initial orientation is critical. Using a compass, align yourself with the cardinal directions (north, south, east, and west) to identify your beginning direction of travel. Identify a conspicuous landmark or feature in the direction you wish to travel and use it as a reference point to keep your bearings during the journey.

3. Using a Luminous or Luminous Compass: Many compasses have luminous or lighted indications that are visible in low-light circumstances. Activate your compass's bright or lit elements to make the directional arrow, degree markers, and bezel visible in the dark. This enables you to obtain bearings, retain directional alignment, and navigate properly despite poor vision.

4. Taking Bearings: To ensure accurate night navigation, precise bearings are required. Using your lighted compass, take bearings on noteworthy landmarks or objects in the environment. Hold the compass steady and level, making sure the magnetic needle aligns with the north indicator or orienting arrow. Take note of the degree reading on the compass bezel, which indicates the landmark's direction relative to your current position.

5. Navigation by Bearings: Once you've taken bearings at significant locations, utilize them to steer your trip. Keep the lit compass in front of you, and match the direction-of-travel arrow or sighting notch to the desired bearing. To travel to the landmark, follow the compass needle's direction. Regularly check the compass to ensure you are heading in the right direction and staying on track.

6. Terrain Association: Terrain association is an important approach for night navigation, particularly in places with low visibility. To augment compass navigation, look for conspicuous landscape features, including ridgelines, valleys, rivers, and other natural landmarks. To validate your location and path, compare the features visible in the terrain to those depicted on the map.

7. Night Sky Navigation: When visibility allows, you can travel using the night sky instead of a compass. Determine cardinal directions by identifying notable stars or celestial entities, such as Polaris (the North Star). Use star patterns and constellations as navigational aids to enhance compass navigation and maintain directional alignment.

8. Maintaining Situational Awareness: For safety and navigation at night, maintaining situational awareness is critical. Stay aware of your surroundings, listening for sounds, and paying attention to changes in terrain. Use your senses to improve compass navigation and safely travel in the dark.

Mastering night navigation using a compass allows outdoor enthusiasts and navigators to effectively travel in low-light or overnight settings, ensuring safe and successful outdoor experiences. Practice these techniques in a variety of settings to improve your nighttime navigation abilities and outdoor experiences.

Inclement Weather

Using a compass in bad weather presents particular problems due to diminished vision, changing ambient circumstances, and potential interference with the compass needle. However, with the right tactics and safeguards, it is still feasible to navigate efficiently in severe weather circumstances with a compass.

Here's a comprehensive discussion of using a compass in adverse weather:

1. Protecting the Compass: In adverse weather, keep your compass away from dampness, rain, snow, and extreme temperatures. When not in use, store the compass in a protective case or bag to keep it safe from the weather. Keep the compass dry and clean to avoid water damage and get accurate readings.

2. Maintaining Visibility: When visibility is low, such as fog, rain, or snow, it is critical to keep the compass needle and markings visible. Use a compass with bright or illuminated indications that are visible in low-light situations. When necessary, illuminate the compass with a torch or headlamp to make the directional arrow, degree markers, and bezel more visible.

3. Taking Bearings: In adverse weather, keep the compass stable and level to obtain accurate readings. To protect the compass from wind and precipitation, cup your palm around it or use a temporary barrier, such as a jacket or cap. Take bearings towards major landmarks or objects visible in the environment, then record the degree reading on the compass bezel.

4. Navigation by Bearings: In inclement weather, use your compass's bearings to guide your travel direction. Hold the compass in front of you, and align the direction-of-travel arrow or sighting notch with the desired bearing. To travel to the landmark or feature, follow the compass needle's direction. Regularly check the compass to ensure you are heading in the right direction and staying on track.

5. Compensating for Declination: During bad weather, it is critical to account for magnetic declination, which is the angular difference between magnetic north and true north. Adjust the compass readings to verify that your navigation is in line with the map's real direction of travel. To make any necessary modifications, refer to the map's declination information or a declination chart.

6. Terrain Association: In addition to the compass, terrain association is an effective tool for navigating in inclement weather. To augment compass navigation, look for conspicuous landscape features, including ridgelines, valleys, rivers, and other natural landmarks. To validate your location and path, compare the features visible in the terrain to those depicted on the map.

7. Maintaining Situational Awareness: During severe weather, situational awareness is critical for safety and navigation. Stay aware of your surroundings, listening for sounds, and paying attention to changes in terrain. Use your senses to enhance compass navigation and securely navigate in inclement weather. Understanding these strategies and safeguards allows outdoor enthusiasts and navigators to efficiently use a compass to navigate in bad weather, ensuring safe and successful expeditions. Practice these techniques in different weather situations to improve your navigation skills and outdoor experiences.

When navigating without visible landmarks, it can be challenging to stay on course.

Navigation without visual markers is difficult, especially in circumstances with poor vision, such as deep woodlands, featureless terrain, or whiteout conditions in snowy areas. In such cases, navigators must use different tactics and approaches to establish their location and travel securely.

Here's a full explanation of navigating without visual landmarks:

1. Compass Navigation: A basic approach for navigating in the absence of visual landmarks. Use a compass to identify your starting direction of travel and keep it steady throughout your journey. Take precise measurements of significant geographical features or distant locations on the map that may not be visible. Use the compass to determine your direction of travel and navigate along your intended itinerary.

2. Dead Reckoning: Dead reckoning is a navigation strategy that involves guessing your position based on your previous known location, direction of travel, and distance traveled. In locations with no visible landmarks, dead reckoning is critical for determining your position and navigating properly. Keep track of your route, mileage traveled, and topographical characteristics encountered to determine your present position on the map.

3. Terrain Association: Terrain association is an effective approach for navigating in situations with no visible landmarks. To augment compass navigation, look for conspicuous landscape features, including ridgelines, valleys, rivers, and other natural landmarks. To validate your location and path, compare the features visible in the terrain to those depicted on the map. Pay attention to variations in landscape, height, and vegetation to spot prospective landmarks or features that might not be obvious from a distance.

4. Using GPS and electronic gadgets: In situations with no visible landmarks, GPS and electronic gadgets may be extremely useful for navigating. Use a GPS device or smartphone with GPS capabilities to get your present location, plan your route, and navigate to waypoints or destinations. However, be careful that GPS signals may be unstable or absent in some situations, such as deep forests or hilly areas with limited satellite view.

5. Celestial Navigation: Celestial navigation uses celestial bodies like the sun, moon, stars, and planets to identify direction and navigate. Celestial navigation may be an effective alternate approach for identifying direction and keeping orientation in areas where there are no visible landmarks. Use the location of celestial bodies relative to the horizon, especially during clear nighttime skies.

6. Using Reference Points: In featureless terrain or situations with no apparent landmarks, using reference points will help you retain orientation and travel more successfully. Create reference points along your path using natural or man-made elements like rock cairns, trail markers, or GPS waypoints. Use these reference points to help you plan your journey and track your progress.

7. Maintaining Situational Awareness: In situations with no visible landmarks, situational awareness is critical for safety and navigation. Stay aware of your surroundings, listening for sounds, and paying attention to changes in terrain. Use your senses to aid navigation and ensure safe passage across featureless areas. By understanding these strategies and procedures, outdoor enthusiasts and navigators can efficiently navigate situations with no visible landmarks, ensuring safe and successful expeditions in difficult terrain. Practice these skills in a variety of settings to improve your navigation and outdoor experiences.

TROUBLESHOOTING AND FAQ

Troubleshooting and frequently asked questions (FAQs) are key components of any compass-related educational material. They address common challenges and concerns that users may have when navigating using a compass and provide solutions.

Here's a full description of troubleshooting and FAQs about compass usage:

1. Compass Calibration Issues: The compass needle sticks or fails to move freely. Solution: Keep the compass level and away from magnetic objects such as metal or electronic equipment. Rotate the compass gently so that the needle settles and aligns with the magnetic north.

2. Declination Adjustments:

Problem: How can I compensate for magnetic declination?
Solution: Use the map's declination information or a declination chart to establish the appropriate adjustment for

your location. Adjust the compass accordingly to ensure that your navigation is true north.

3. Interference from External Sources

Problem: Nearby electrical gadgets or metal items interfere with compass readings.

Solution: Move away from electrical gadgets and metal items to reduce interference with the compass needle. Make sure the compass is level and away from any potential sources of interference.

4.Night Navigation:

Problem: How can I travel by compass at night?

Solution: To increase visibility in low-light conditions, use a compass with bright or lighted markers. To improve sighting of the directional arrow and degree marks, illuminate the compass with a flashlight or headlamp as needed.

5. Lost bearings: Issue: I have lost my bearings. How do I know what my present job is? Solution: To identify important landmarks or features in the landscape, use terrain association techniques. Take bearings on these features and use them to get your approximate position on the map.

6. Compass Accuracy:

Problem: How can I verify the correctness of my compass readings?

Solution: Calibrate the compass on a regular basis and make sure it is level and steady when obtaining readings. Cross-reference your data with observable geographical features and landmarks to ensure their correctness.

7. Weather conditions:

Problem: How can I navigate with a compass in inclement weather?

Solution: Keep the compass away from moisture and severe temperatures to ensure reliable readings. Use terrain association and dead reckoning to travel efficiently in limited visibility or bad weather.

8. Using Compass with Maps:

Problem: How do I use a compass and maps to navigate?
Solution: Align the map with magnetic north and use the

compass to take bearings on noteworthy sites or features shown on the map. Use these bearings to determine your direction of travel and navigate your chosen path. These troubleshooting tips and FAQs address frequent problems and issues that users may have while using a compass to navigate. Understanding these answers and practicing good compass usage skills allows users to travel comfortably and effectively in a variety of situations and conditions.

Common Mistakes

How to Avoid Them Common compass navigation errors can cause erroneous readings, loss of direction, and difficulties reaching your goal. By recognizing these typical mistakes and how to prevent them, navigators may enhance their compass abilities and navigate securely in a variety of situations.

Here's a comprehensive list of frequent errors and how to avoid them:

1. Incorrect Compass Holding: Holding a compass improperly might result in false readings. Avoid twisting or angling the compass, since this might cause the needle to stick or swing randomly. To ensure accurate readings, keep the compass level and stable, parallel to the ground.

2. Failure to Calibrate the Compass: Not calibrating the compass might lead to erroneous readings. Before using the compass, make sure the magnetic needle is in line with the orienting arrow or north indication. Rotate the compass housing until the needle settles and points to the north magnetic field.

3. Forgetting to correct for declination: Failure to correct for magnetic declination might result in navigational mistakes. Always adjust compass readings for the local declination angle shown on a map or declination chart. This guarantees that your navigation remains true to the north and does not deviate from your desired path.

4. Failure to Orient the Map: Using a map without first orienting it to magnetic north might lead to confusion and inaccuracies. Always use a compass to align the map with magnetic north. This ensures that your map appropriately depicts the topography and the direction of travel.

5. Inaccurate Bearing Readings: Taking incorrect bearing readings might result in navigation mistakes. When taking bearings, keep the compass stable and level, and line up the direction-of-travel arrow or sighting notch with the intended landmark or feature. Before you proceed, double-check the bearing reading to guarantee its correctness.

6. Overreliance on the Compass: Using the Compass without cross-referencing with other navigation aids or procedures might result in inaccuracies. In conjunction with the compass, use terrain association, dead reckoning, and other navigation tools to confirm your position and direction of travel. This adds redundancy and improves navigation accuracy. External interference from adjacent electrical gadgets or metallic objects can affect compass readings. Be aware of potential sources of interference, and keep the compass away from such items to reduce inaccuracies. To check the accuracy of your readings, cross-reference them with observable geographical characteristics.

7. Lack of Practice: Insufficient practice and familiarity with compass use might result in errors and uncertainty during navigation. To develop confidence and skill, practice using the compass in a variety of settings and situations on a regular basis. To enhance your navigation abilities, become familiar with various compass approaches and practice fixing frequent difficulties. Navigators can navigate securely and efficiently using a compass in a variety of locations if they recognize the frequent pitfalls and adopt strategies to prevent them. To ensure safe and effective outdoor trips, use correct compass procedures, keep watchful, and strive to develop your navigation abilities on a constant basis.

Troubleshooting Compass Issues

Troubleshooting compass difficulties is a necessary skill for outdoor lovers and navigators to guarantee precise and dependable navigation. A variety of variables can influence compasses, resulting in inaccuracies in readings or operations.

Here's a full description of typical compass problems and how to solve them:

1. Debris or dirt may impede the movement of the compass needle if it is stuck or unresponsive. To resolve this issue, gently tap or spin the compass housing in a circular motion to remove any debris that may be causing the needle to stick. If the needle remains stuck, thoroughly wipe the compass

housing and needle with a soft cloth to remove any dirt or debris.

2. Metal Object Interference: Nearby metal objects can disrupt the magnetic field, causing erroneous compass readings. To solve this problem, avoid metal items like automobiles, buildings, or fences that could interfere with the compass. Hold the compass away from your body and any metal items to avoid interference and guarantee precise readings.

3. Erroneous calibration: If the compass needle does not align with the orienting arrow or north indication during calibration, it may indicate an erroneous calibration. To fix this problem, keep the compass level and away from magnetic objects while calibrating. Slowly rotate the compass housing until the needle has settled and aligned with the orienting arrow. If the calibration is still faulty, recalibrate the compass in a new area to reduce interference.

4. Declination Adjustment Problems: Incorrect magnetic declination adjustments might result in navigational problems and inaccurate compass readings. To troubleshoot this issue, use the map's declination information or a

declination chart for your specific location. Adjust the compass accordingly to ensure that your navigation is true north. Double-check the declination adjustment to guarantee accuracy and avoid deviating from the intended direction.

5. Low Visibility of Markings: In low-light settings or at night, compass markings may be difficult to read. To resolve this issue, use a compass with bright or lighted indications that are visible in low light. When necessary, illuminate the compass with a torch or headlamp to make the directional arrow, degree markers, and bezel more visible.

6. Compass misalignment may occur if the compass is not kept level or if the user's hand interferes with the movement of the needle. To solve this issue, keep the compass level and stable, parallel to the ground, for accurate readings. To avoid interfering with its movement, keep your hand away from the compass housing and needle.

7. Magnetic Deviation: Errors in compass readings caused by magnetic objects or electrical equipment in close proximity. To resolve this issue, walk away from electrical gadgets and metal items that may be interfering with the compass. Hold the compass away from your body and any

potential sources of interference. Addressing compass difficulties, outdoor enthusiasts and navigators may assure precise and dependable navigation in a variety of locales and situations. To avoid problems and assure peak performance during outdoor expeditions, use correct compass usage skills, remain watchful, and examine and repair your compass on a regular basis.

Frequently Asked Questions

Outdoor lovers, hikers, and explorers benefit greatly from knowing how to navigate using a compass. However, users may have difficulties or issues with how to use a compass efficiently.

Here are some commonly asked questions (FAQs) and responses to common concerns:

1. Why is my compass needle stuck or not moving freely? The compass needle may become stuck as a result of magnetic interference from surrounding items, such as metal or electronics. Hold the compass away from such items and in a level position so that the needle may travel freely.

2. How should I correct for magnetic declination?

Magnetic declination refers to the angular difference between magnetic north and true north. To compensate for magnetic declination, use the declination information on the map or a declination chart for your region. Adjust the compass readings to correspond with true north.

3. What should I do if adjacent electronic gadgets or metal items interfere with my compass readings?

Stay away from electronic gadgets and metal items to avoid interference with the compass needle. Hold the compass firm and level to guarantee accurate readings, and cross-check your results with obvious landscape characteristics.

4. How can I travel using a compass at night or in low-light conditions?

Use a compass with bright or lighted markers to improve vision in low-light environments. To improve sighting of the directional arrow and degree marks, illuminate the compass with a flashlight or headlamp as needed.

5. What should I do if I've lost my bearings and need to find my present location?

To identify important landmarks or features in the landscape, use terrain association techniques. Take bearings on these features and use them to get your approximate position on the map. Adjust your route based on the updated bearings.

6. How can I verify the correctness of my compass readings? Calibrate the compass on a regular basis, and keep it level and stable when obtaining readings. Compare your readings to observable geographical features and landmarks to see if they are accurate.

7. What other navigation methods may I use in addition to a compass?

In addition to a compass, you may utilize terrain association, dead reckoning, celestial navigation, and GPS devices to navigate. Familiarize yourself with various navigation strategies and try utilizing them in diverse settings.

8. What should I do if I encounter bad weather when traveling with a compass?

Keep the compass away from moisture and severe temperatures to guarantee reliable readings. Use terrain association and dead reckoning to travel efficiently in limited visibility or bad weather. By answering these frequently asked questions, users can overcome typical obstacles and confidently navigate with a compass in a variety of outdoor settings. To improve your outdoor experiences, use accurate compass skills and remain up-to-date on navigation concepts.

Compass Care and Maintenance

A compass requires proper care and maintenance to maintain accuracy, dependability, and lifespan. Users may keep their compass in good working order by following a few easy rules.

Here's a thorough explanation of compass care and maintenance:

1. Storage: When not in use, keep the compass in a case or bag to protect it from dust, moisture, and potential damage. Avoid keeping the compass near powerful magnetic fields or electrical gadgets that might interfere with the magnetic needle.

2. Cleaning: Clean the compass on a regular basis to eliminate dirt, dust, and debris that might interfere with its operation. Wipe the bezel, crystal, and compass housing with a gentle, dry cloth. Avoid using strong chemicals or abrasive cleansers, which might harm the compass.

3. Avoiding Impact: Handle the compass with care and avoid dropping or impacting it, since this can harm the casing, crystal, and internal components. To avoid unintentional damage, always store the compass in a secure position while not in use.

4. Calibration: To obtain accurate readings, calibrate the compass on a regular basis. Calibration entails matching the magnetic needle with the orienting arrow, or north indication. Rotate the compass housing until the needle settles and points to the north magnetic field. Repeat this technique on a regular basis, particularly if the compass readings appear to be wrong.

5. Protection against Moisture: Keep the compass away from moisture, water, and severe humidity to avoid harm to its internal components. Avoid exposing the compass to rain, snow, or water immersion, and if it does become wet, completely dry it. Keep the compass in a dry place to avoid moisture buildup.

6. Checking for Damage: Inspect the compass on a regular basis for signs of damage or wear, such as cracks, scratches, or loose parts. To ensure that the magnetic needle travels

smoothly without sticking, check its alignment. Address any problems right away to avoid further damage and keep the compass accurate.

7. Battery Replacement (for lighted compasses): If your compass has luminous or illuminated markings powered by batteries, change them as needed to maintain visibility in low-light settings. To prevent compass damage, follow the manufacturer's battery replacement instructions and only use compatible batteries.

8. Professional Maintenance: If your compass requires more than basic maintenance, contact a professional compass technician or a manufacturer-authorized service shop. Do not attempt to disassemble or repair the compass yourself, as this may void the warranty or cause additional damage. Regular maintenance and good handling will enable users to move confidently and securely during their outdoor experiences.

Properly storing your compass is essential

Proper compass storage is critical for maintaining accuracy, protecting it from damage, and ensuring its longevity.

Here's a comprehensive look at how to properly store a compass:

1. Protective Case or Bag: When not in use, keep the compass in a protective case or bag. This serves to protect the compass from dust, grime, moisture, and potential damage. Many compasses come with a protective case or bag when purchased, but if not, consider purchasing one to keep your compass safe while in storage.

2. Dry Environment: Keep the compass in a dry place to avoid moisture buildup, which can harm the internal components and reduce its accuracy. Avoid keeping the compass in wet or humid environments, such as basements or bathrooms, since extended exposure to moisture can cause corrosion and malfunction.

3. Away from Strong Magnetic Fields: Keep the compass away from magnets, electronic equipment, or metal items that cause strong magnetic fields. Strong magnetic fields can interfere with the compass needle, affecting calibration and accuracy.

4. Keep the compass away from magnetic objects: Keep the compass in a secure location that won't be damaged by collision or accident. Avoid placing heavy objects on top of the compass or leaving it in a location where it could be knocked over or dropped. Store the compass in a drawer, shelf, or compartment that will not be bumped or jostled.

5. Avoid extreme temperatures: The compass should not be kept at extreme temperatures because heat and cold can impair its performance. High temperatures can cause the fluid-filled capsule to expand, resulting in incorrect readings, while low temperatures can cause the fluid to contract, altering the movement of the magnetic needle. To avoid temperature variations, store the compass in a climate-controlled environment.

6. Regular Inspection: On a regular basis, check the compass for signs of damage, wear, or corrosion. To ensure that the magnetic needle travels smoothly without sticking, check its alignment. Address any problems right away to avoid further damage and keep the compass accurate. By following these storage rules, users can protect their compass from harm, ensure its accuracy, and extend its lifespan. Proper storage is critical for keeping a dependable and accurate compass for navigation on outdoor trips.

Tips for Cleaning and Maintaining

Cleaning and maintenance are critical to sustaining a compass's accuracy, dependability, and lifetime.

Here are some cleaning and maintenance methods to maintain your compass in top condition:

1. Regular Cleaning: Clean your compass on a regular basis to remove any dirt, dust, or debris that may have accumulated on its surface. Wipe the bezel, crystal, and compass housing with a gentle, dry cloth. Avoid using abrasive cleansers or strong chemicals, since these can harm the compass.

2. Avoid Moisture: Keep your compass dry and protected from moisture, since water can harm the internal components and reduce its accuracy. If your compass becomes wet, gently dry it with a soft towel and let it air dry before storing it.

3. Protective Case: When not in use, keep your compass in a protective case or pouch to keep it safe from dust, grime, and damage. Many compasses come with a protective case or bag when purchased, but if not, consider purchasing one to keep your compass safe while in storage.

4. Avoid severe temperatures: Protect your compass from severe temperatures, since both hot and low temperatures might impair its operation. High temperatures can cause the fluid-filled capsule to expand, resulting in incorrect readings, while low temperatures can cause the fluid to contract, altering the movement of the magnetic needle. To avoid temperature swings, keep your compass in a climate-controlled area.

5. Calibration: You should calibrate your compass on a regular basis to guarantee accurate readings. Calibration entails matching the magnetic needle with the orienting arrow, or north indication. Rotate the compass housing until the needle settles and points to the north magnetic field.

Repeat this technique on a regular basis, particularly if the compass readings appear to be wrong.

6. Inspect for Damage: On a regular basis, check your compass for any signs of damage, wear, or corrosion. To ensure that the magnetic needle travels smoothly without sticking, check its alignment. Address any problems right away to avoid further damage and keep the compass accurate.

7. Battery Replacement (if applicable): If your compass has luminous or illuminated markings powered by batteries, replace them as needed to maintain visibility in low-light conditions. To prevent compass damage, follow the manufacturer's battery replacement instructions and only use compatible batteries.

8. Professional Maintenance: If your compass requires more than routine maintenance, contact a professional compass technician or a manufacturer-authorized service center. Do not attempt to disassemble or repair the compass yourself, as this may void the warranty or cause additional damage. Follow these cleaning and maintenance tips to keep your compass in top condition for precise navigation on your outdoor adventures. Regular maintenance is required to ensure the reliability and longevity of your compass.

Checking for accuracy

Checking the accuracy of your compass is critical for safe navigation during outdoor activities.

Here are some steps that will help you check the accuracy of your compass.

1. Calibration: Check your compass's accuracy before using it. Calibration entails matching the magnetic needle with the orienting arrow, or north indication. Rotate the compass housing until the needle settles and points to the north magnetic field. Repeat this process on a regular basis, especially if you suspect the compass readings are inaccurate.

2. Comparison with Known Directions: Bring your compass to a location with known directions, such as a trail marker or sign indicating north, south, east, or west. Hold the compass level and steady, then compare the needle's direction to the known directions. Check that the compass accurately aligns with the expected cardinal directions.

3. Cross-Reference with Map: If possible, compare your compass readings to features on a map. Using your compass, align the map with magnetic north and compare the compass needle's direction to the map's features. Check that the compass readings correspond to the map features and terrain.

4. Repeat Readings: Using your compass, take multiple readings from various locations and compare them. Ensure that the readings are consistent and follow the expected directions. If there are any discrepancies between readings, calibrate the compass and repeat the process to ensure accuracy.

5. Terrain Association: Use terrain association techniques to ensure the accuracy of your compass readings. Identify prominent landmarks or features visible in the terrain, and use your compass to determine their bearings. To confirm accuracy, compare the compass bearings to the terrain's actual features.

6. Back Bearings: Take back bearings to previously passed features or landmarks. This allows you to ensure that your compass readings match known features and verify your position along the route.

7. Professional Verification: If you are concerned about the accuracy of your compass or notice persistent discrepancies in readings, seek professional verification from a compass technician or a manufacturer-authorized service center. They can conduct a thorough inspection and calibration to ensure the compass is accurate. By following these steps, you can ensure that your compass is accurate and that you can navigate reliably while outdoors. Regularly checking the accuracy of your compass is critical for safe and successful navigation in a variety of environments.

BEYOND THE BASICS

Advanced Compass Tools Beyond the basics of compass navigation, there are advanced tools and techniques that can help you improve your navigational skills and capabilities. These advanced compass tools aim to enhance navigation accuracy, especially in challenging or intricate terrain.

Here's a detailed look at some advanced compass tools:

1. Clinometer: A clinometer is a built-in feature in some advanced compass models or is available as a separate accessory. It determines the terrain's slope or inclination angle. Using compass bearings and slope measurements, navigators can accurately assess the steepness of terrain and plan routes accordingly. Clinometers are especially useful when navigating mountainous terrain or areas with significant elevation differences.

2. Sighting Mirror: An advanced compass may include a sighting mirror, which helps you take precise bearings on distant landmarks or features. The sighting mirror allows users to align the compass with the target while simultaneously viewing along the mirror's reflected line of sight. This allows for more accurate bearings, particularly over long distances or in open terrain where landmarks may be distant or obscured.

3. Global Needle: Some advanced compass models include a global needle, which remains steady and accurate regardless of where you are on Earth. Unlike traditional compass needles, which can tilt or wobble near the magnetic poles, a global needle is stable and provides accurate readings even in Polar Regions. This feature is especially useful for navigators exploring high latitudes or Polar Regions, where traditional compasses may be unreliable.

4. Declination Adjustment Mechanism: While basic compasses require manual adjustment for magnetic declination, advanced compasses frequently have a built-in mechanism for automatic or simple adjustment. This enables users to set the compass to the appropriate declination angle for their location, ensuring that their navigation is in line with true north without the need for manual calculations or adjustments.

5. Multiple Scales and Units: Advanced compasses may have multiple scales and units of measurement, such as degrees, mils, or gradations, to accommodate various navigation techniques or preferences. This versatility enables users to switch between scales and units as needed, based on specific navigational tasks or requirements.

6. Altimeter: Some advanced compass models have an altimeter that measures altitude or elevation above sea level. Altimeter readings are useful for navigating mountainous terrain, locating your position on a topographic map, and estimating elevation changes along your route. This feature improves navigation accuracy and situational awareness, particularly in rugged or vertical terrain.

7. GPS Integration: In addition to traditional compass functions, some advanced compasses include GPS technology to improve navigation capabilities. GPS integration enables users to track their location, record waypoints, and navigate with digital maps and satellite positioning data. This combination of compass and GPS functionality offers comprehensive navigation tools for outdoor adventures in a variety of settings. Mastering these advanced compass tools and techniques allows navigators to confidently and accurately navigate difficult terrain and diverse outdoor environments. Advanced compasses provide increased functionality and precision, allowing users to navigate more confidently and efficiently during outdoor adventures.

Using a Compass Clinometer

A compass clinometer, also known as a clinometer compass, is a specialized tool for determining slope angles or inclinations in terrain. It combines the functions of a compass and a clinometer, allowing users to determine the steepness of terrain and plan routes accordingly. The clinometer feature is especially useful for hikers, mountaineers, and other outdoor enthusiasts who are navigating mountainous or hilly terrain and require precise slope measurements for safety and route planning.

To use a compass clinometer, take the following steps:

1. Activate the Clinometer: To begin, activate your compass's clinometer feature. Depending on the model, this may entail flipping a switch, rotating a dial, or adjusting a lever to activate the clinometer.

2. Hold the Compass Level: Keep the compass level and steady, parallel to the ground. This is critical for taking accurate slope measurements, as holding the compass at an angle can result in incorrect readings.

3. Align the Compass: Position the compass on the slope or incline you want to measure. Hold the compass in front of you, and point the clinometer scale (usually located on the side or bottom of the compass housing) at the slope. A clinometer scale typically consists of a series of markings indicating degrees or percentages of slope. After aligning the compass with the slope, read the measurement displayed on the clinometer scale. This measurement represents the terrain's slope or inclination angle with respect to the horizontal plane.

4. Interpret the measurement: Use the measurement to determine the terrain's steepness. Angle measurements will be higher on steeper slopes and lower on gentler slopes. Use this knowledge to make sound decisions about route selection, navigation, and terrain negotiation.

5. Repeat as needed: Measure multiple slopes at various points along your route to gain a thorough understanding of

the terrain's topography. This allows you to identify areas with varying steepness and plan your route accordingly, avoiding steep or dangerous terrain.

6. Adjust Route Planning: Use the slope measurements from the compass clinometer to modify your route planning and navigation strategy. Avoid routes with excessively steep slopes, which may pose a safety risk or necessitate excessive physical exertion. Instead, choose routes with more manageable slopes that match your skill level and objectives.

7. Practice and Familiarization: In a variety of terrain conditions, use the compass clinometer to become familiar with its operation and accurately interpret slope measurements. Regular practice will help you assess the steepness of terrain and make informed decisions on outdoor adventures. Outdoor enthusiasts can use a compass clinometer to accurately assess terrain steepness, improve route planning, and navigate safely and confidently through mountainous or hilly terrain.

 Understanding how to use this specialized tool is critical for adventurers who want to confidently and proficiently explore rugged landscapes and challenging environments.

Combining GPS with Compass Navigation

Incorporating GPS technology with compass navigation can significantly improve navigational capabilities, giving users comprehensive tools for precise and efficient navigation in a variety of outdoor environments. By combining the strengths of compass and GPS systems, users can benefit from the accuracy of compass bearings and the real-time positioning data provided by GPS satellites.

Here's a detailed overview of integrating GPS and compass navigation:

1. GPS Positioning: The GPS (Global Positioning System) technology uses satellite signals to determine the user's precise location on Earth's surface. GPS receivers calculate the user's latitude, longitude, and elevation using signals received from multiple satellites orbiting the Earth. This real-time positioning data gives users accurate information about their current location, allowing them to precisely pinpoint their position on a map.

2. Compass Bearings: Compass navigation uses magnetic bearings to determine the direction of travel in relation to magnetic north. By applying compass bearings to visible landmarks or features, users can establish their orientation and navigate along their planned route. Compass bearings offer a dependable way to determine direction, particularly in environments where GPS signals may be obstructed or unavailable.

3. Cross-Reference: To integrate GPS with compass navigation, cross-reference GPS coordinates with compass bearings. Users can use GPS positioning data to identify their current location on a map and then take compass bearings to nearby landmarks or features to confirm their orientation and direction of travel. This cross-referencing technique enhances navigational accuracy by combining GPS positioning with compass bearings.

4. Waypoint Navigation: GPS devices allow users to set waypoints, which are specific coordinates marking key locations along a route or trail. By setting waypoints at strategic points on a map, users can navigate to these locations using GPS positioning data. Users can use compass bearings along with GPS waypoints to verify their direction of travel and confirm alignment with the planned route.

5. Navigational Aids: GPS devices often include built-in navigational aids such as digital maps, route planning tools, and track logs. Users can use these features to plan routes, mark waypoints, and track their progress along a route in real time. Compass navigation complements GPS features by providing a backup method for determining direction and orientation, especially in situations where GPS signals may be unreliable or obstructed.

6. Situational Awareness: Incorporating GPS with compass navigation enhances situational awareness by providing users with multiple sources of navigational information. GPS positioning data offers real-time location tracking, while compass bearings provide a reliable method for determining the direction of travel. By combining these sources of information, users can navigate with confidence and make informed decisions during their outdoor adventures.

7. Backup Navigation: GPS devices are susceptible to signal interference, battery depletion, or technical malfunctions, which may affect their reliability. In such situations, compass navigation serves as a valuable backup method for navigating without relying solely on GPS technology. Users who carry both a GPS device and a compass have redundant navigation tools to ensure they can navigate effectively in any situation. Incorporating GPS with compass navigation offers users a powerful combination of navigational tools, providing accuracy, reliability, and versatility for navigating in various outdoor environments.

Compasses in Specialized Fields (e.g., Aviation, Marine)

Compasses play critical roles in various specialized fields, including aviation, marine navigation, and military operations, where precise navigation is essential for safety, efficiency, and mission success.

Here's a detailed overview of compasses in specialized fields:

1. **Aviation Compasses:** In aviation, pilots use traditional magnetic compasses as primary or backup navigation instruments. They provide pilots with a reliable reference

for determining the aircraft's heading relative to magnetic north. Magnetic compasses are crucial for maintaining directional awareness, especially in situations where other navigation instruments may fail or experience technical issues.

Remote Indicating Compasses (RMI) in modern aircraft display magnetic heading information on cockpit instruments. Pilots benefit from accurate heading information provided by RMIs, which can be integrated with other navigation systems to enhance situational awareness and precision navigation.

2. **Gyroscopic Compass:** Gyroscopic compasses, also known as directional gyros or heading indicators, are gyroscopic instruments that provide heading information based on gyroscopic principles. Gyroscopic compasses provide stable and accurate heading references, particularly during aircraft maneuvers or turbulent conditions where magnetic compasses may be subject to errors.

3. **Marine Compasses/ Magnetic Compass:** In marine navigation, magnetic compasses are fundamental

instruments used for determining a vessel's heading relative to the magnetic north. They provide sailors with essential directional information for plotting courses, navigating channels, and maintaining course corrections. Vessels often integrate magnetic compasses into their navigation systems and complement them with other electronic navigation aids.

4. **Gyrocompasses are specialized compasses** used in marine navigation to provide accurate and stable heading references based on gyroscopic principles. Unlike magnetic compasses, gyrocompasses are unaffected by magnetic variations or disturbances and provide reliable heading information even in polar regions or near magnetic anomalies.

5. **Large vessels and ships**: Commonly use gyrocompasses for critical navigation and maneuvering requiring precise heading information.

6. **Fluxgate Compass:** Fluxgate compasses are electronic compass systems used in marine navigation to provide accurate heading information based on magnetic field measurements. Fluxgate compasses are compact, lightweight, and less susceptible to magnetic

interference compared to traditional magnetic compasses. Navigation systems on smaller vessels, yachts, and recreational boats often integrate them for accurate heading reference and navigation assistance.

7. **Military Compasses/ Lensatic Compass:** Lensatic compasses, also known as military compasses or marching compasses, are rugged and durable compasses used by military personnel for land navigation, reconnaissance, and tactical operations. They feature a foldable design with a sighting lens and a floating magnetic dial for precise navigation and target acquisition.

8. **Prismatic Compass:** Prismatic compasses are specialized compasses used in military applications for artillery targeting, surveying, and reconnaissance. They feature a prism and sighting system for accurate aiming and measurement of azimuths, angles, and bearings. Prismatic compasses are versatile instruments used by military units for navigation, reconnaissance, and tactical planning. Compasses in specialized fields such as aviation, marine navigation, and military operations are critical tools for ensuring accurate navigation, safety,

and operational effectiveness in diverse environments and conditions. These compasses meet the unique requirements and challenges of their respective fields, providing users with reliable and precise navigation capabilities.

REAL-WORLD APPLICATIONS OF COMPASSES

The real-world applications of compasses are diverse and span across various fields, from outdoor recreation to professional industries.

Here's a detailed overview of some real-world applications of compasses:

1. Outdoor Recreation

Hiking and Backpacking Compasses: are essential tools for hikers and backpackers navigating trails and wilderness areas. They provide reliable direction and orientation, helping outdoor enthusiasts stay on course and find their way in unfamiliar terrain.

Orienteering: Orienteering is a popular outdoor sport that involves navigating through checkpoints using a map and compass. Compasses are indispensable for orienteers as they plot routes, take bearings, and navigate accurately through forests, hills, and other natural landscapes.

Geocaching: Geocaching is a recreational activity that involves using GPS coordinates to locate hidden containers, or "geocaches," in outdoor environments. Compasses complement GPS devices by providing directional assistance and helping geocaches navigate to precise locations within a designated area.

2. Professional Industries

Professionals in surveying and cartography use compasses to determine direction, measure angles, and establish reference points for mapping and land surveying projects. They are essential tools for professionals working in land surveying, topographic mapping, and geographic information systems (GIS).

Compasses in construction and engineering lay out building sites, align structures, and determine directional bearings for infrastructure projects.

They aid construction workers, engineers, and architects in maintaining accurate alignment and orientation during building construction and development. Compasses play a role in forestry and natural resource management by assisting professionals in conducting field surveys, marking boundaries, and navigating through forested areas. They are useful tools for foresters, environmental scientists, and conservationists working on forestry management and land conservation projects.

3. **Navigation and transportation:** Compasses are critical tools in aviation and marine navigation for determining direction, setting courses, and maintaining headings during flight and maritime operations. Pilots, sailors, and navigators rely on compasses for accurate navigation and course corrections, especially in situations where other navigation systems may be unavailable or unreliable.

4. **Search and Rescue Operations:** Compasses are used in search and rescue operations to navigate through rugged terrain, track search patterns, and coordinate rescue efforts. Search and rescue teams rely on compasses as essential tools for guiding search operations and locating missing or stranded people in remote areas.

5. Military and Defense

Military Operations: Compasses are essential tools for military personnel conducting land navigation, reconnaissance, and tactical operations. Military compasses provide accurate direction and orientation for soldiers navigating through challenging terrain, planning maneuvers, and executing missions in the field. Compasses in artillery targeting and fire control systems calculate azimuths, angles, and bearings for accurate aiming and targeting of artillery weapons.

Military compasses aid artillery units in adjusting fire and directing artillery rounds towards designated targets with precision and effectiveness.

Compasses have diverse real-world applications across various fields, from outdoor recreation and professional industries to navigation and defense. They are indispensable tools for navigating, orienting, and surveying in both recreational and professional settings, providing users with reliable direction and orientation in diverse environments and conditions.

Wilderness Navigation

Wilderness navigation refers to the art and science of finding one's way through remote and often unmarked terrain using a variety of navigational tools and techniques. It is an essential skill for outdoor enthusiasts, adventurers, and professionals who venture into wilderness areas for hiking, backpacking, mountaineering, or other outdoor activities.

Here's a detailed overview of wilderness navigation:

1. Map reading and interpretation: Wilderness navigation begins with understanding and interpreting topographic maps, which provide detailed information about the terrain, elevation, and features of the wilderness area. Map reading skills include identifying landmarks, contour lines, elevation changes, and other geographical features that aid in navigation.

2. Compass Navigation: Compasses are indispensable tools for wilderness navigation, providing directional assistance and orientation in the absence of visible landmarks or GPS signals. To navigate wilderness terrain accurately, compass navigation techniques include taking bearings, plotting courses, orienting maps, and triangulating positions.

3. Terrain Association : Terrain association involves using visual cues and features in the landscape to navigate through wilderness terrain. By observing and interpreting natural features such as ridgelines, valleys, rivers, rock formations, and vegetation patterns, navigators can orient themselves and navigate in relation to the surrounding terrain.

4. Dead Reckoning: One estimates their current position in dead reckoning based on a previously known position, combined with information about distance traveled, direction, and speed of travel. It entails tracking movement using a compass, pacing, or other methods, as well as maintaining a mental or written record of the route taken to navigate through wilderness areas.

5. GPS Navigation: Global Positioning System (GPS) devices are valuable tools for wilderness navigation, providing precise location data, waypoint marking, and route tracking capabilities. GPS navigation complements traditional map and compass techniques, offering real-time position tracking and navigation assistance, especially in areas with limited visibility or challenging terrain. 6. Route Planning and Preparation: Before venturing into wilderness areas, navigators should engage in thorough route planning and preparation. This includes studying maps, identifying potential hazards or obstacles, planning alternative routes, estimating travel times, and packing essential navigation tools and equipment.

7. Safety and Emergency Preparedness: Wilderness navigation also involves safety considerations and emergency preparedness. Navigators must have emergency communication devices, first aid supplies, navigation backups, and knowledge of emergency procedures for accidents, injuries, or getting lost in the wilderness.

8. Environmental Awareness: Wilderness navigation requires environmental awareness and respect for natural surroundings. Navigators should practice Leave No Trace principles, minimize environmental impact, and adhere to wilderness regulations and guidelines to preserve the integrity of wilderness areas for future generations

Orienteering Competitions

Orienteering competitions are outdoor navigation events that challenge participants to navigate through a series of checkpoints or control points, known as "controls," using only a map and compass. These competitions test participants' navigation skills, physical fitness, and strategic decision-making abilities as they navigate through diverse terrain and varying levels of difficulty.

Here's a detailed overview of orienteering competitions:

1. Format and Structure: Orienteering competitions typically consist of a series of courses, each with its own set of controls. Courses vary in length and difficulty to accommodate participants of all ages and skill levels. Participants navigate from control to control in the correct sequence, punching a card or electronic device at each control to verify their visit. Courses may include various types of terrain, such as forests, parks, urban areas, and mountains, and can range from short sprints to long-distance races lasting several hours.

2. Types of Courses: Sprint courses are short-distance races held in urban or park settings, requiring quick decision-making and precise navigation through complex environments with many route choices.

Middle Distance: Middle distance courses are intermediate-length races held in forested terrain, challenging participants with a mix of navigational and physical demands over varied terrain.

Long Distance: Long distance courses are endurance races held in rugged terrain, testing participants' navigation skills and stamina as they navigate through challenging terrain and varying elevations. Score-O courses are time-limited events where participants must visit as many controls as possible within a set time, choosing their own route and strategy to maximize their score.

3. Competitive Categories: Orienteering competitions typically feature competitive categories based on age, gender, and skill level, allowing participants to compete against others in their respective categories. Categories may include juniors, seniors, masters, and veteran age groups, as well as separate categories for male and female competitors.

4. Equipment: Participants are required to carry essential orienteering equipment, including a map, compass, whistle, punch card, or electronic timing device. Electronic timing devices, like SportIdent or Emit systems, often record participants' times and control visits electronically, offering accurate and efficient timing data for scoring purposes.

5. Scoring and Timing: Scorers evaluate participants according to their completion time and the number of controls they visit in the correct sequence. Electronic timing systems record participants' start and finish times as well as the time taken to visit each control, providing accurate and detailed timing data for scoring purposes.

6. Navigation and Strategy: Success in orienteering competitions depends on effective navigation skills, route choice, and strategic decision-making. Participants must analyze the terrain, plan their routes, and make quick decisions about the most efficient paths to each control, taking into account factors such as distance, elevation, vegetation, and terrain features.

7. Safety and Rules: Orienteering competitions prioritize safety and follow strict rules and guidelines to ensure participants' well-being. Rules may include mandatory equipment requirements, boundary restrictions, time limits, and safety precautions to minimize risks and promote fair competition.

8. Community and Social Aspects: Orienteering competitions foster a sense of community and camaraderie among participants, providing opportunities for social interaction, teamwork, and mutual support. Competitors often share experiences, tips, and strategies with fellow orienteers, building friendships and connections within the orienteering community.

Geocaching with a Compass

Geocaching with a compass adds an additional layer of challenge and adventure to the popular outdoor activity of geocaching, which involves using GPS coordinates to locate hidden containers, or "geocaches," in outdoor environments.

Incorporating a compass into geocaching provides an alternative method for navigation and adds an element of traditional outdoor exploration.

Here's a detailed overview of geocaching with a compass:

1. Navigation Tool: A compass is a traditional navigation tool that provides directional assistance in determining the general direction of a geocache location. While GPS devices offer precise coordinates, a compass can complement GPS navigation by providing a backup method for orienting oneself and navigating towards the geocache.

2. Initial Orientation: Geocachers can use a compass to orient themselves in the general direction of the geocache location before setting out on their adventure. By aligning the compass needle with magnetic north or using other orientation techniques, geocachers can establish their initial bearing and direction of travel towards the geocache.

3. Terrain Association: Once geocachers have established their initial orientation, they can use terrain association techniques in conjunction with the compass to navigate towards the geocache location. By observing natural landmarks, vegetation patterns, and other terrain features, geocachers can navigate towards the geocache using the compass as a directional guide.

4. Dead Reckoning: Geocachers can employ dead reckoning techniques with the compass to estimate their progress and adjust their route towards the geocache location. Geocachers can navigate towards the geocache by tracking their movement, taking periodic compass bearings, and estimating the distance traveled using a combination of compass navigation and dead reckoning.

5. Triangulation: Geocachers can use triangulation techniques with the compass to refine their navigation towards the geocache location. By taking compass bearings to prominent landmarks or features visible from their current location, geocachers can triangulate their position on the map and determine the direction of the geocache relative to their position.

6. Additional Challenges: Geocaching with a compass introduces additional challenges and complexity to the activity, as it requires geocachers to rely on traditional navigation skills and techniques. It encourages outdoor enthusiasts to develop their compass navigation skills, spatial awareness, and environmental observation skills while engaging in the adventure of geocaching.

7. Backup Navigation: Using a compass as a backup navigation tool provides geocachers with redundancy and reliability in case of GPS device failure or signal loss. It ensures that geocachers can continue their adventure and navigate towards the geocache location, even in challenging or remote outdoor environments where GPS signals may be unreliable. In conclusion, geocaching with a compass offers outdoor enthusiasts a unique and rewarding way to explore the great outdoors while honing their traditional navigation skills. By incorporating a compass into the geocaching activity, participants can enjoy the adventure of searching for hidden treasures while embracing the challenges and excitement of traditional outdoor exploration.

Conclusion

The compass is a timeless and indispensable tool for navigation in both outdoor adventures and specialized fields. From its humble origins as a magnetic needle floating in water to its modern iterations with advanced features, the compass has remained a reliable guide for determining direction and orientation in diverse environments.

Throughout this exploration, we've delved into the fundamental principles of compass navigation, understanding its components, calibration, and various techniques for accurate navigation. We've also explored advanced compass skills, such as using clinometers, incorporating GPS technology, and navigating challenging terrain. Moreover, we've seen how the compass finds applications across a wide range of fields, including outdoor recreation, professional industries, navigation, and defense. Whether it's guiding hikers through rugged landscapes, aiding sailors in charting courses across vast oceans, or assisting military personnel in tactical operations, the compass continues to play a vital role in facilitating safe and efficient navigation. Furthermore, we've examined how the compass adds an extra dimension to recreational activities like geocaching, offering enthusiasts an opportunity to hone their navigation skills while embarking on thrilling outdoor adventures. In essence, the compass stands as a symbol of exploration, adventure, and discovery, guiding us through the unknown and enabling us to navigate with confidence in an ever-changing world.

As we embrace new technologies and innovations, let us not forget the timeless wisdom and reliability embodied by this simple yet indispensable tool: the compass.

www.ingramcontent.com/pod-product-compliance
Lightning Source LLC
LaVergne TN
LVHW051655050326
832903LV00032B/3830